Young and Wild

Contents

Joey Grows Up

Written by Jack Kimble

Australia

Joeys are baby kangaroos. They live in Australia. Can you find Australia on a world map?

Joey is born!
He is very little.
He is as little
as a bee.
He has no fur.

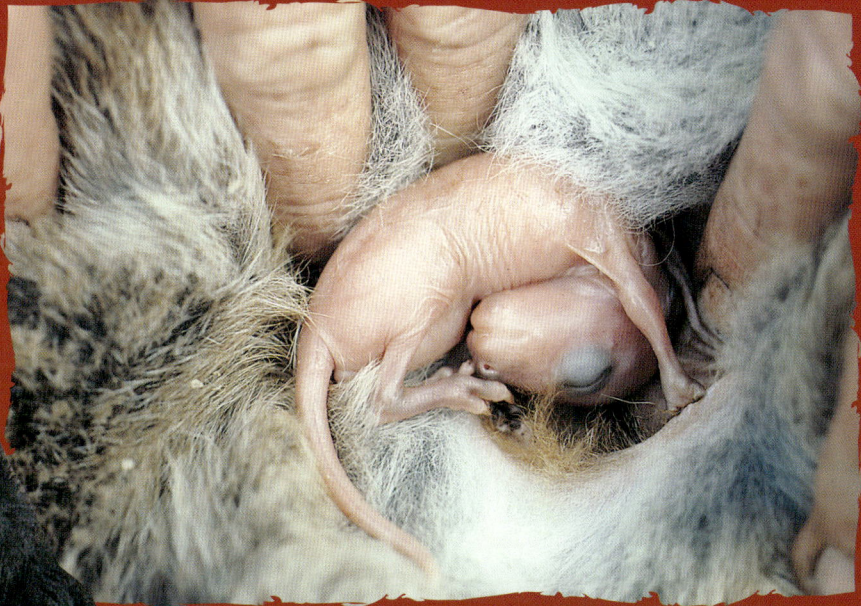

With tiny claws,
he climbs into
his mother's pouch.
There he rests.
He drinks milk.
And he grows.

Joey looks out
of his mother's pouch.
He is much bigger now.

Joey's mother eats grass.
Joey is hungry, too.
Joey eats some grass.

Joey always
has a ride!

It is warm in the pouch.
It is safe in the pouch.
But Joey wants to move!
He climbs out.
He wobbles.
He hops!

Dingoes
are wild dogs.
Sometimes dingoes
attack kangaroos.

Watch out, Joey!
Some dingoes are near.
Joey is scared.
He quickly climbs back
into his mother's pouch.

Look at the time line below and see a joey grow.

Joey likes to play.
He plays
with his brother.
This is how
he learns to fight.

Newborn

5 months

Joey is too big
for the pouch now.
But he stays by
his mother.

When he is two years old,
he can live
on his own.

7 months

12 months

Boo to You

Bert

Gert

Written by Carrie Waters   Illustrated by Chris Mousdale

Bert and Gert were bear cubs.
Bert liked to ride on his sled
and make things.
Gert liked to ride on her sled
and scare Bert.

Once. Gert painted her nose white.

Where did
that rock
come from?
I can have
some fun
with it.

One day,
Gert saw Bert go out.

Gert hid
by the rock.

The rock got up.

Boo to you!

Gert ran.
She didn't stop until
she was under her bed.

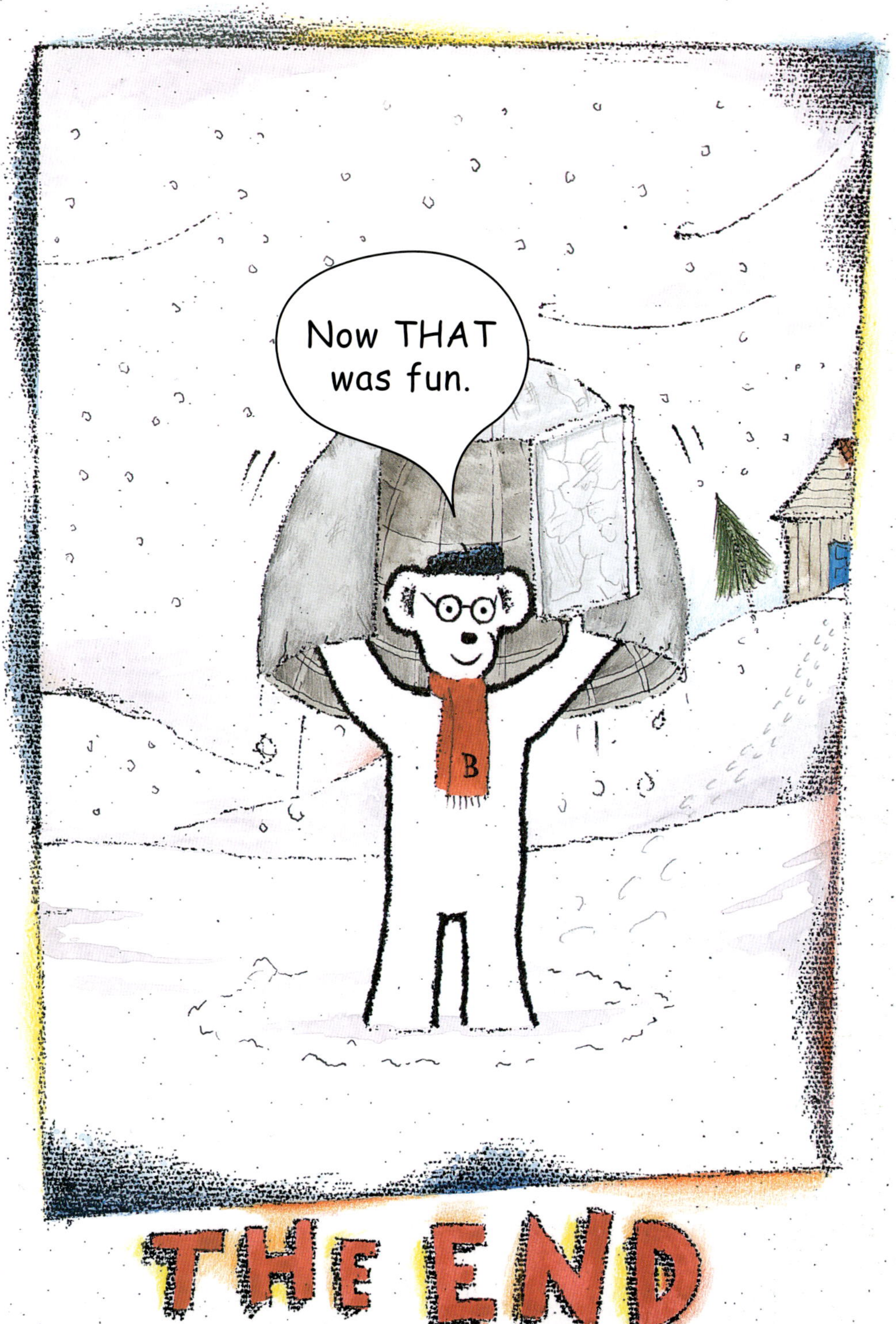

THE END

Animal Dads

Written by Laura Hirschfield

Animal babies need lots of care. Most of the time, animal mums care for their babies alone. But some animal dads take care of babies, too.

A midwife toad dad looks after his eggs until they hatch.

This dad takes care
of his babies before
they are born.

Mum lays eggs
in a special pouch
in his belly.
The eggs hatch
inside his belly.

After they hatch,
he pushes out
the babies
one by one.
He can have up to
300 babies at once!

Sea horse dad with a baby

This dad takes care
of an egg, too.
He keeps the egg
on top of his feet.
Brrrr! It is cold.
He covers the egg
with his belly skin
to keep it warm.

He does not eat.
He does not walk.
He waits about 60 days
for the egg to hatch.
When the chick is born,
its mum brings food
for it to eat.

Emperor penguin dads and chicks

This dad takes care of twins!
When they are born,
their dad holds them.
He cleans them.
He grooms their fur.

This marmoset dad carries
his babies on his back.

Marmoset dad and babies

Most marmosets have twins!

As the twins grow up, Dad helps feed them. He helps teach them how to crawl. He helps teach them how to take care of themselves.

23

This dad takes care of Mum and the pups.
Mum stays in the den with the pups.
Dad keeps them safe from hungry animals.
He brings them food.

As the pups grow up, he plays with them.
He teaches them how to hunt.
He teaches them
how to stay safe.

Red fox parents look after their babies together.

This red fox is feeding its pup.

Did you know some red foxes are not red? They can be black or silver.

So you see, animal mums aren't the only ones to take care of babies. Some animal dads have lots of work to do, too!

Fly with the Birds

Written by Linda Johns

Illustrated by Meng-Feng Wu

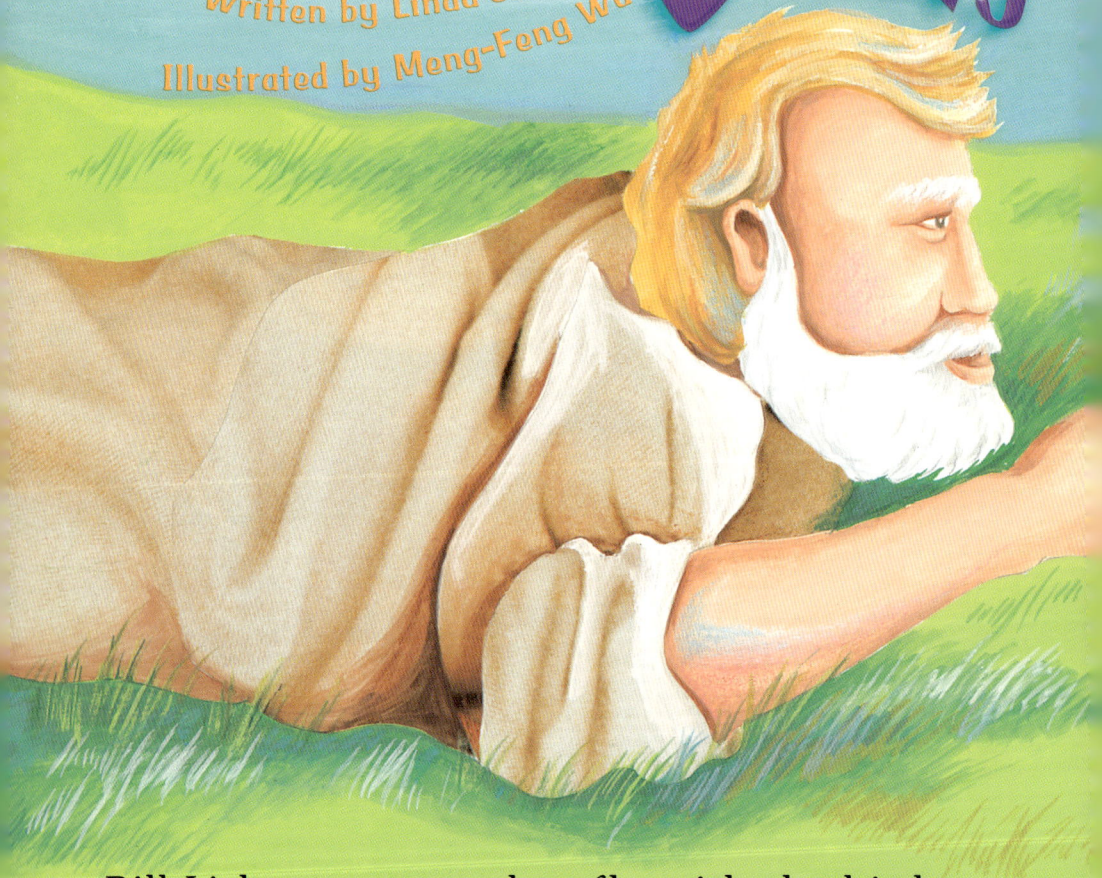

Bill Lishman wanted to fly with the birds.
He wanted to be the first person
to fly with geese.

Gosling is the word for a baby goose.

Baby geese learn fast.
They start to learn soon
after they come out of their eggs.

But who teaches baby geese to fly?
Does it have to be a mother goose?
Does it have to be a father goose?
Does it have to be a goose?
Bill knew that it did not.

Bill found some goose eggs.
The eggs hatched.
The goslings came out.
They saw Bill.

When goslings are born,
they follow the first thing they see.
The goslings followed Bill.
They swam with him.
They ran with him.
He was their leader!

Now Bill wanted to teach them to fly.
First he ran.
He ran faster and faster.
He got on a motorcycle
and went even faster.
The geese ran.
They started to flap their wings.

Some people call Bill Lishman "Father Goose".

Next, Bill got in an aeroplane.
He flew the aeroplane.
The geese flew, too.
Bill was their leader.
He was flying with the birds!

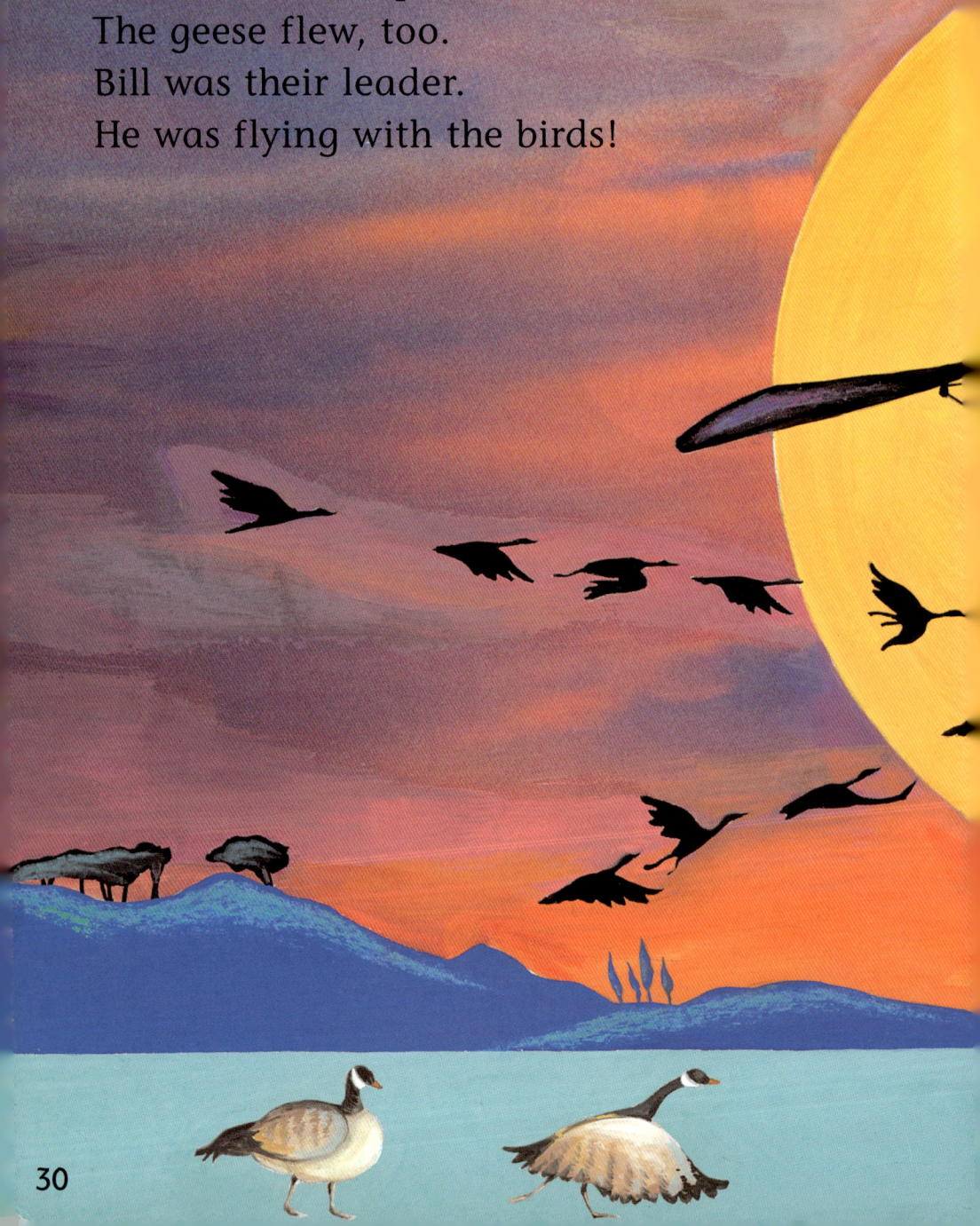

Bill Lishman was the first human to fly in formation with birds. He flew with a flock of Canada geese. He used what he learned to help lead other flocks of birds south for the winter.

Why do you think birds would need Bill's help to fly south?

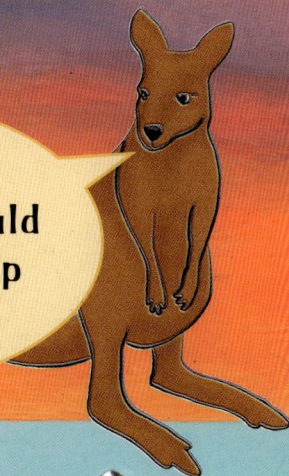

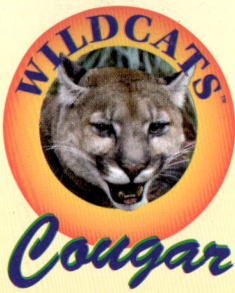

Index